A QUINTET BOOK

Published by Chartwell Books
A Division of Book Sales, Inc.
PO Box 7100
Edison, New Jersey 08818-7100

This edition produced for sale
in the U.S.A., its territories
and dependencies only.

ISBN 0-7858-0316-5

This book was designed and produced by
Quintet Publishing Limited
6 Blundell Street
London N7 9BH

Creative Director: Richard Dewing
Designer: James Lawrence
Project Editor: Anna Briffa
Editor: Lydia Darbyshire
Photographer: Paul Forrester

Typeset in Great Britain by
Central Southern Typesetters, Eastbourne
Manufactured in Singapore by Eray Scan Pte Ltd
Printed in China by Leefung-Asco Printers Ltd

ACKNOWLEDGMENTS

The author would like to thank the following
people for the loan of their artwork:
Alex Douglas Morris, Adrianne Cross,
Charles Penny and Jim Russel

CONTENTS

INTRODUCTION

Framing is a wonderful craft, and one of its great appeals is that it takes so little time to learn how to make a simple frame. With only a couple of pieces of wood and some glass you can make a present for a friend or a frame for a favorite photograph that is ready to hang on the wall within minutes.

Once you have mastered the basic techniques, you will find that there are endless possibilities, and the time taken perfecting the various aspects of the craft is very satisfying. The frame is important because any picture needs to be confined within a clearly defined area. When there is no frame, the eye tends to wander and it is difficult to focus on the image and to appreciate it properly. It is essential that the frame enhances the picture without overpowering it. The finishing edge – that is, the mount and the frame – should complement the picture but they must never be so intrusive that they are the first thing you look at. The frame is there to protect the work and to give it its own space within its surroundings. The finishing edge must ensure that the eye travels easily to the focal point of the picture.

There are no hard and fast rules that must be observed when you are choosing colors for the mounts and moldings. Some people seem to have a knack for selecting the perfect combinations of shades; others learn as they go along. You may find it helpful to visit art galleries, museums and shops to look at the ways different frames and moldings can be used to create different effects and how the various materials can be used to enhance the pictures they surround. If you look at Victorian watercolors, for example, you will see how the overall balance is maintained by the use of light ivory or cream-colored mounts, often decorated with wash lines, together with a fairly dark wooden or deep gold frame. In general, a dark mount will look best with a lighter frame. Photographs, for instance, look good in smaller, darker mounts, with a narrow aluminum or silver-colored frame. Traditional framing has a long and rich history, but new products, which make techniques such as gilding and distressing so much easier than they used to be, have changed people's attitudes to the craft and encouraged new fashions. For example, at present a wood and paint finish is popular, and this technique is explained later in the book.

EQUIPMENT AND TECHNIQUES

You need only a few tools to get started and you can even begin, as I did, by working on the sitting-room floor. If you are lucky, you will find that you already have most of the tools and equipment you will need in your household tool cupboard. There are, however, two items that you will probably have to buy – a miter box (or clamp) and a mount cutter – but, in general, you should think about buying new tools only as you need them, rather than acquiring them all at once.

FRAMING

To make the frames described in this book you will need the following:

◊ Pin hammer
◊ Tenon saw
◊ Screwdriver
◊ Pincers/pliers
◊ Nail punch
◊ Set square
◊ Hand drill and bits

◊ Panel pins
◊ Miter box or clamp
◊ Metal ruler
◊ Plastic ruler and pencil
◊ Craft knife
◊ Wood glue

MOLDINGS

There is an enormous range of moldings available to the amateur framer these days, but the main problem is finding shops that supply what you need and want. Some manufacturers operate a mail-order service, and you will find their names and addresses in craft magazines. A timber merchant may keep a few moldings in stock, and your local picture framer may also be persuaded to help. When you are choosing a molding, consider the size of the picture and such aspects as whether it is boldly colored or finely drawn.

Because hard wood has become much scarcer in recent years, plastic moldings have been introduced. These have the great advantages that they do not warp or suffer from woodworm. They also take gilding and colored finishes well, although they do not, of course, have the wonderful smell and feel of real wood.

MOLDING FORMULA

• This simple formula can be used to work out fairly accurately how much molding you will need. Add together:

The height of the picture x 2
The width of the picture x 2
The width across the top of the frame (ie of the molding) x 8

You need the additional width of the molding for the miter cuts that are made at the ends of each of the four pieces.

For example, say that you are framing a picture measuring 12 x 10in and that the depth of the molding is ½in:

12in x 2 = 24in
10in x 2 = 20in
½in x 8 = 4in
= 48in

Add an extra 2in to be on the safe side, and this means that you will need 50in in total.

USING THE CLAMP AND SAW

When your saw is new you may find that a little oil will make it run smoothly when you are cutting molding. Try not to put a lot of pressure on the saw when you are cutting. Aim to use short, light, even strokes and to let the saw do the work. When it is not being used, always keep the saw in its cover to protect the teeth.

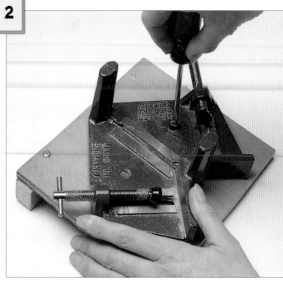

1 The clamp needs to be fixed to a wooden base. You will need a piece of ⅛in plywood measuring about 8 x 7in. Cut a length of 1⅛ x 1in timber to 8in and screw it along the longer side of the piece of plywood to form a lip that will butt up against the edge of your working surface.

2 Screw the metal miter clamp onto the plywood base so that the lip is on the other side.

3 Before you use a clamp for the first time, you may find it helpful to draw a line on the rubber insert of the base of the clamp to indicate the central cutting line.

USING A MITER CLAMP

- Make sure that the molding is sitting flat on the base before you tighten up the screws.
- Use small pieces of card or off-cuts of wood at the end of the clamp screws to protect the molding from any damage.
- If the base moves around too much when you are sawing pieces of wood, use a clamp to hold the base firmly to your working surface.
- When you have cut a corner and you need to smooth the edges, gently rub the cut edge on the rough side of some hardboard instead of using sandpaper, which may be too severe.

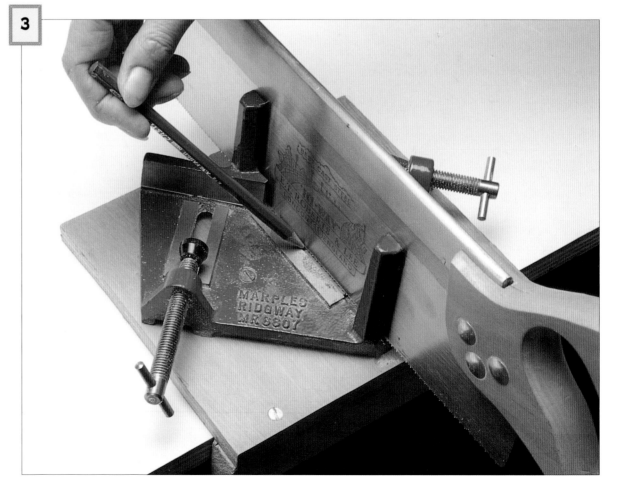

USING CORNER CLAMPS

Frame corner clamps held with a cord are available, although they can be rather fiddly and awkward to work with. They can be useful, however, especially if you are making small or very narrow frames that are difficult to pin.

Take the four cut pieces of the frame and glue the ends of the long sides. Lay the frame on your working surface in the correct position and put the four corner clamps in place. Pull up the string until it is very tight, clean off any glue that has seeped out from the joints and put to one side until the glue is dry. There are several different types of frame corner clamps available.

MOUNTING

Your choice of mount can affect the final appearance of the painting even more than the frame itself. If the mount is too small it can appear to squeeze and confine the picture, so, at least at first, you should always make the mount slightly larger than you had originally planned.

You will need the following equipment to make the mounts described in this book:

◊ Cutting mat
◊ Mount cutter with ruler
◊ Compasses
◊ Pencil
◊ Adhesive tape
◊ Plastic ruler and pencil
◊ Scissors
◊ Craft knife
◊ Mapping pen and paint brush

You must make sure that the blade of your mount cutter is sharp. Keep a supply of spare blades and replace the worn one as often as necessary, but certainly every 5 or 6 mounts. Dispose of the old blade carefully.

Remember that the bottom edge of the mount is usually deeper than the top and sides, which should be the same depth. For example, if the top and sides were 3½in deep, the bottom should be 4in deep. This difference helps to lead the eye into the picture.

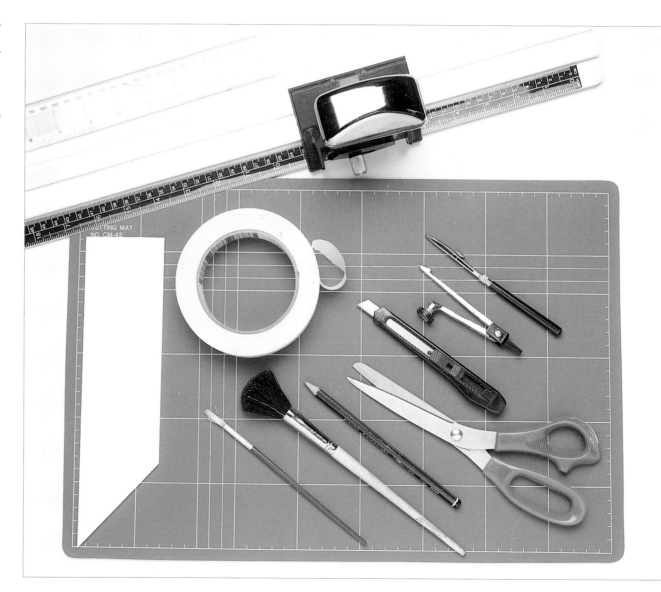

There is a huge range of mounting boards and cards available – the selection is so wide, in fact, that it can be rather confusing.

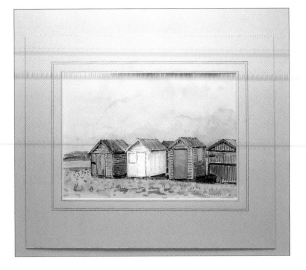

In general you should choose a light color, especially if you are framing a watercolor painting. Pick an appropriate color from the painting itself and match the tone of the color with a light green, soft brown, ivory, cream and so on. If the color seems too bland when it is surrounding the picture, wash or crayon lines can be added to draw the eye to the painting. A brightly colored painting may look best with a pale mount but with a more vividly colored frame.

There are several kinds of mount, and it is important to select the appropriate kind for the image you are framing. The different types are:

◊ A normal window mount
◊ A double mount, in which about ⅛in of the color of the underlying mount can be seen around the edge of the top mount
◊ A float, in which the picture lies on a colored mount with 1–1¼in) of the mount showing all round the edge of the picture
◊ A float and mount combined, in which the picture lies on the lower mount while the window in the top mount is cut to reveal ½–¾in of the bottom mount around the picture
◊ Fabric covered mounts, when silk or hessian is used over the mount
◊ Paper-covered mounts
◊ Wash mounts

These are just a few of the possible mounting methods and materials. If you take care with the mount, choosing it thoughtfully and cutting it precisely, it will make all the difference to the final look of the picture.

Being sepia, this photograph has been treated like a drawing, and so has a large mount. Generally, however, they can often look swamped if the mount is too large, and they generally look best in small, dark mounts.

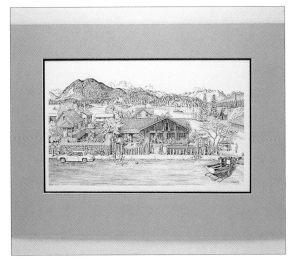

Prints require special treatment. If they are original, they will have a plate mark impressed on the paper, all around the image. The window of the mount should be sufficiently large for the plate mark to be visible, which usually means leaving a margin of white about ⅛in wide around the actual printed image.

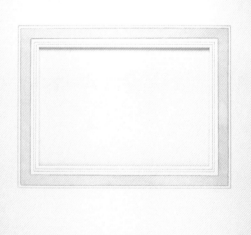

TIP

- Your choice of mounting technique can radically alter the final appearance of the picture or photograph, as can be seen from this picture, which has been mounted in three different ways.

  A normal window mount
  A float
  A double mount

CUTTING A MOUNT

Select a suitable color of mounting card. We are mounting a brightly colored painting, which needs a quieter colored mount so that the painting stands out. We later added a colored frame, which tied the scheme together. In addition to the mounting card of your choice, you will need:

◊ Cutting board (see page 11)
◊ Scraps of card
◊ Sharp pencil and ruler
◊ Set square
◊ Mount cutter
◊ Craft knife or razor blade
◊ Backing board
◊ Masking tape
◊ Acid-free tape (optional)

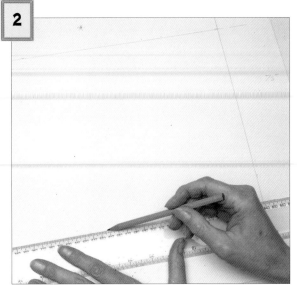

1 Measure the picture and decide on the area you want to show in the window of the mount. For this picture the window is going to be 13 x 9½in. The width of the mount at the top and both sides will be 3in and the width at the bottom will be 3⅛in. Therefore, to calculate the total area of mount add the width of the window to twice the width of the side and add the depth of the window to the top and the bottom widths of the mount. In our example, that is 13 + 6in, which gives an overall width of 19in, and 9½ + 3 + 3⅛in, which gives an overall depth of 16in.

2 Lay the cutting board on a flat surface and place some scrap card on it. On the reverse side of the mounting card draw a rectangle to the outside dimensions of the mount – in our example this is 19 x 16in. Use a set square to make sure that the corners are exactly 90 degrees. Cut out the mount area.

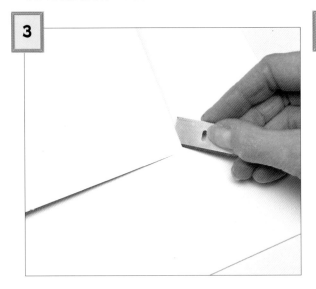

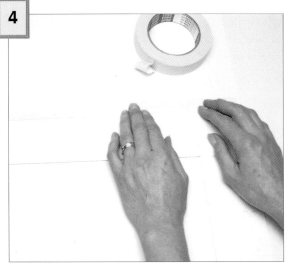

3 Again on the reverse side, draw the window opening. Measure in from the outside edge, in this case 3in from the top and sides, and 3⅛in from the bottom. Cut the window. If the window does not fall out easily, use a sharp craft knife or razor blade to finish the corners. Make sure that they are clean and neatly cut.

4 Cut a piece of backing board the same size as the outside dimensions of the mount and lay the mount face down beside the backing board, with the long edges abutting. Use small pieces of masking tape to hold the top edges together. This hinges the mount and the backing board together.

5 Open out the mount and backing board and lay the picture on the backing board. Bring the mount over the picture and adjust the position of the picture. If your picture is not valuable, hold it in position under the edge of the mount with masking tape; a more valuable picture should be held with acid-free tape. Cut two pieces of tape and hold the picture in place at the top with these. Cut two further pieces of tape and cover the top ends of the tape to make sure that it is securely held.

USING THE MOUNT CUTTER

You should follow the instructions that come with your mount cutter, but the following guidelines apply to all makes.

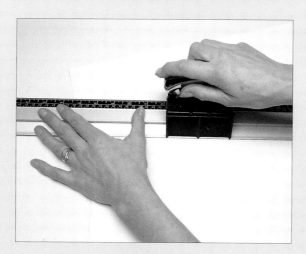

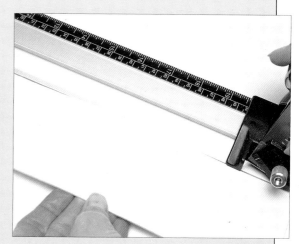

• Make sure that the blade is sharp and that it is set so that it just cuts through the mounting card and into the scrap card beneath.

• Lay the ruler so that the blade follows the pencil line. Insert the blade just beyond the corner and pull it toward you, finishing just beyond the corner nearest to you.

• Test to see if the cut is clean. Keeping the ruler in position, lift the edge of the card to check that the cut has gone right through. If it has not, slide the cutter down the line again.

Remember that, when you have completed each cut, you should move the scrap card so that the blade does not get stuck in the groove made by the first cut.

HANGING MATERIALS

You will need a range of rings and eyes to provide secure hangers for your finished frames. The specific items are listed with each project, but you are likely to need some or all of the following:

◊ D-rings
◊ Screw eyes
◊ Wire or cord
◊ Metal glass clips
◊ Plastic mirror clips
◊ Brown adhesive paper
  or masking tape

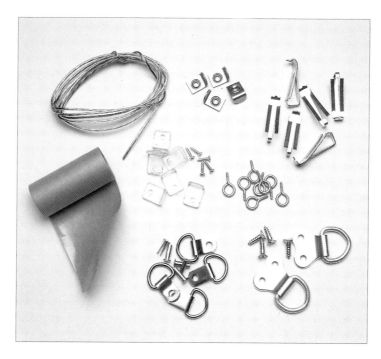

MAKING A CUTTING SURFACE

• Although you can buy special cutting mats in craft and art material shops, they are not cheap and they are, in any case, available in only a limited range of sizes. You can easily make your own, which will provide a suitable surface for cutting both the mounts and the glass and which can be almost any size you wish.
• To make a cutting surface measuring about 30 x 36in, which is large enough for most frames, cut a piece of hardboard and a piece of mounting card to the same size. Use an ordinary rubber-based adhesive to stick the mount to the shiny side of the hardboard, or, if you have one, use a staple gun to fix the two pieces together. The card will wear down eventually and need to be replaced, but this is not difficult.
• Always place a piece of scrap card between the mount you are cutting and the surface of your cutting board, and remember to move the waste card after each cut so that the blade does not stick in the groove and cause the cut to become ragged.

CUTTING GLASS

Glass cutting is much easier than you may think, and unless your frame is very large you should be able to cut glass to fit all your frames. You will need the following equipment:

◊ Glass cutter
◊ Wooden T-square or squaring ruler
◊ Pincers
◊ Felt-tipped pens

Buy a good glass cutter. The better quality the cutter, the easier your work will be. The best kind have a little built-in reservoir to hold white spirit or glass-cutting oil, which keeps the cutting head clean and running smoothly. If your cutter does not have this feature, you will need to dip the head into white spirit before each cut.

Picture frames take 1/16in glass, which you can buy in small quantities from your glass merchant and which is much thinner and lighter than the glass used for windows. Buy a few off-cuts in the beginning so that you can practice your cutting technique.

A flat surface is absolutely essential. You can use a cutting mat or make a cutting surface as explained on page 11.

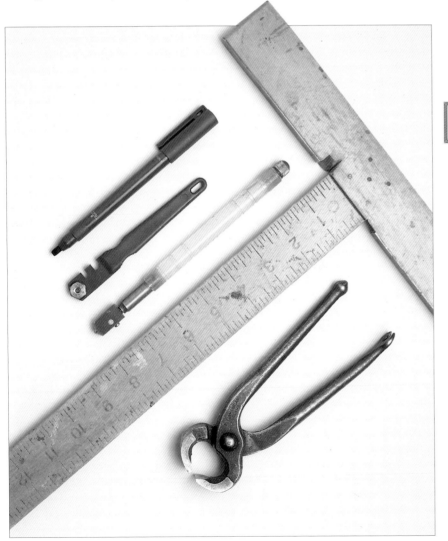

CUTTING GLASS TO SIZE

1 Lay a small piece of glass on the flat surface and hold your cutter between your first and second fingers, supporting it with your thumb so that it is almost upright. If you find this uncomfortable, you can hold the cutter between your thumb and first finger.

2 Practice scoring the glass. Do this a few times on different parts of some spare glass until you feel comfortable with the cutter and you can hear the satisfying sound that indicates that you have cleanly scored the glass every time. Throw away this piece of glass.

3

3 Put another piece of glass on your working surface. Lay the cross end of your T-square against the top of the glass so that the long piece is flat on the surface of the glass with the top edge butted up against the edge of the glass. Take your glass cutter and, pressing down firmly, pull it down one side of the T-square. Do not go over the scored line a second time or you will damage the cutter.

4

4 Carefully raise the glass at one side and slide the ruler under the cut, so that the edge of the ruler is exactly under the scored line.

5

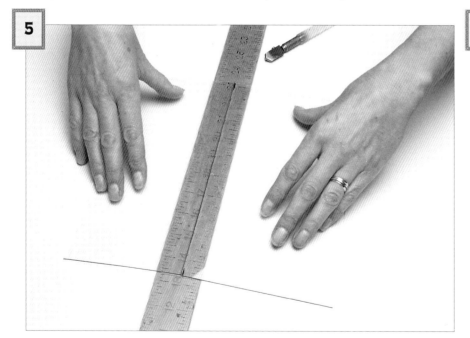

5 Place the fingertips of each hand on either side of the ruler and press down sharply. If your cut was good, the glass will break easily.

6

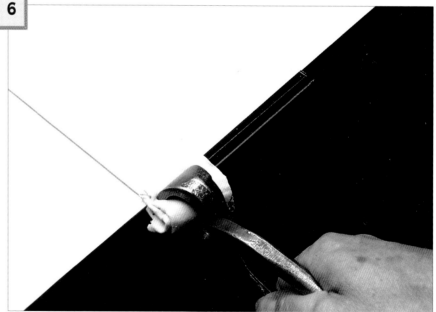

6 If the glass does not break smoothly or if you need to cut a small sliver from the edge, place the glass so that the edge of your work surface aligns with the scored line (which you may, for once, need to go over with your cutter for a second time). Put a piece of cloth in the jaws of your pliers or pincers, grip the edge of the glass and snap it off.

BASIC FRAME

This first frame is for a print of a colorful Mediterranean scene which looks good with white space around it. It will be framed to the edge of the paper without a mount. The molding is fairly wide wood, which is easier to work with than narrow, flexible molding – it is also easier to correct mistakes on wood.

You will need

◊ Molding (see page 5 for estimating quantity)
◊ Miter cutter and clamp
◊ Saw
◊ Plastic ruler and pencil
◊ Wood glue
◊ Drill and fine bit
◊ Panel pins
◊ Small hammer
◊ Nail punch
◊ ⅛in glass
◊ T-square
◊ Felt-tipped pen
◊ Glass cutter
◊ ⅛in hardboard
◊ Metal ruler
◊ Craft knife
◊ D-rings or screw eyes
◊ Masking tape
◊ Brown adhesive paper
◊ Wire or cord

1 Make the first miter cut by sliding the molding into the left side of the miter cutter so that the screw clamp butts against the back of the frame. Protect the molding with card or off-cuts of wood and screw the clamp firmly.

1

2

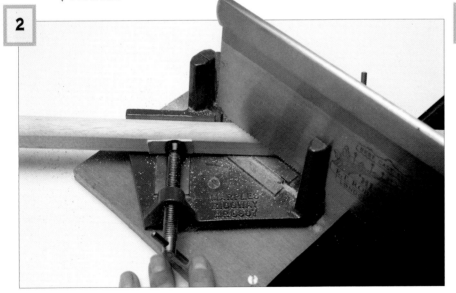

3

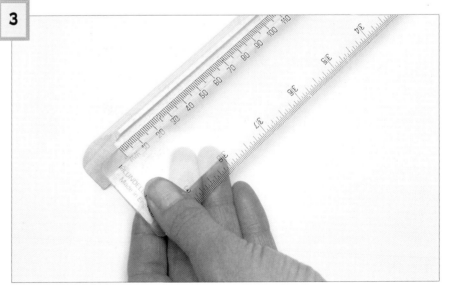

2 Gently push the nose of the saw into the slit that is nearest to you and slide it into the further slit. Without putting a lot of pressure on the wood, slide the saw backward and forward, using small, even strokes. Do not tilt the saw.

3 Unclamp the molding and lay it on your working surface with the rebate side toward you. Working on the longest dimension first, use your ruler to measure from the inside of the corner you have just cut and mark the required length.

4 Slide the molding into the right side of the miter corner – that is, the opposite side from your first cut – and push the molding along until your pencil mark is on the center line of the miter cutter.

5 Clamp and cut it as the other side. Put the finished piece to one side.

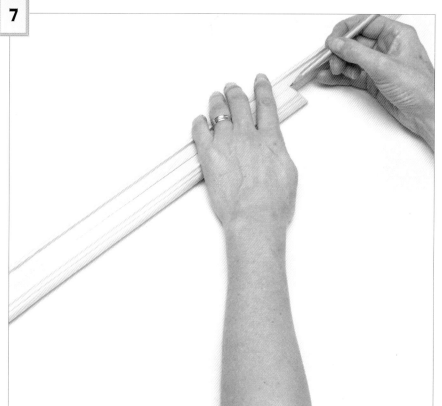

6 You now have to make a new 45-degree angle on the remaining piece of molding by cutting off the waste. Slide the molding into the left side of the clamp, screw it tightly in place and cut the new angle.

7 Measure the second long side. Place the first piece you cut so that it is back to back with the second piece. Carefully line up the corners and mark the length of the first piece on the back of the second piece. Slide the molding into the right side of the clamp, line up your mark with the center line of the clamp, tighten and cut.

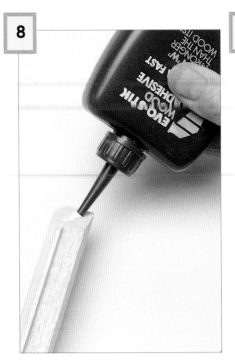

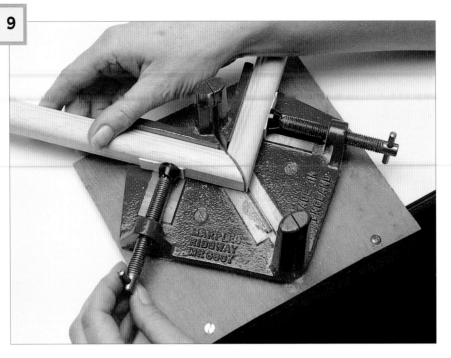

8 Repeat steps 3–7 to make the two short sides. Then take a long piece and a short piece and put some wood glue on the corner angle of the long piece.

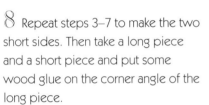

9 Place the two pieces, corner to corner, in the clamp, adjust and readjust until they fit neatly and tightly together and are firmly held.

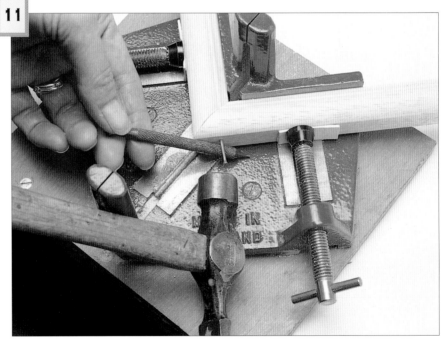

10 Use a drill with a fine bit to make small holes for the panel pins. When you lay a panel pin across the corner it should be long enough to penetrate well into the other piece. A 1in pin is usually long enough, but if you are using wide molding you may need 2in pins.

11 Hammer the pins in gently, using a punch to help drive the pins home. A punch is especially useful if the wood is hard. Repeat the steps for the opposite corner, making sure that the second long piece goes into the clamp on the same side as the first. You can now glue and pin the final corners to complete the frame. If you are going to paint your frame, this is the time to do so.

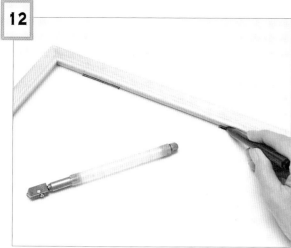

12 Cut the glass by transferring the dimensions of the picture to the glass with a felt-tipped pen, and lining your T-square against the marks before cutting on the inside of the marks by about ⅛in to allow for the width of the head of your glass cutter. Alternatively, simply lay the frame on the glass at a corner so that the frame butts up to the edges of the glass. Use a felt-tipped pen to mark the edges that are sitting on the glass and cut as before.

13 Lay the piece of glass on the hardboard and draw around it so that it is exactly the same size as the cut glass.

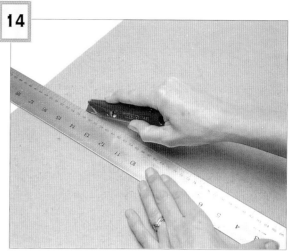

14 Lay a heavy metal ruler along the line and draw the blade of your craft knife down the line several times. Do not press too hard – you are not cutting right through the hardboard but scoring it. With the ruler held in the same position, sharply pull up one side of the hardboard. It should snap cleanly. If it does not, align the scored line with the edge of your working surface and snap it downward.

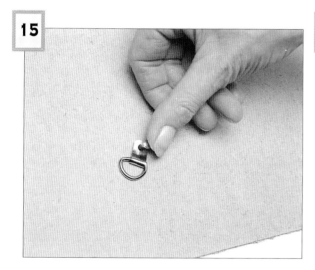

15 Mark positions for two D-rings on the hardboard – these should be about one-third of the way down and 2–2⅛in in from the sides – and use a nail punch (or bradawl) and hammer to make the holes.

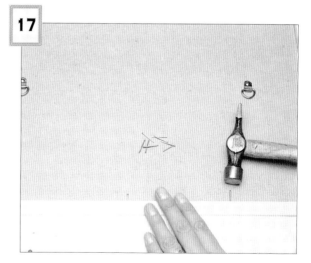

16 Place the D-rings in place and push through the rivets. Turn over the hardboard and, resting it on a flat surface, split open the rivets with a screwdriver and hammer them flat. Cover the rivets with small pieces of masking tape.

17 Sandwich the hardboard and glass together with the picture between them. Lay the components on your working surface and place the frame around them. Pick the whole piece up and turn it over. Hold the back in the frame by driving in a few small panel pins. Lay the pins on the hardboard and tap them carefully into the frame.

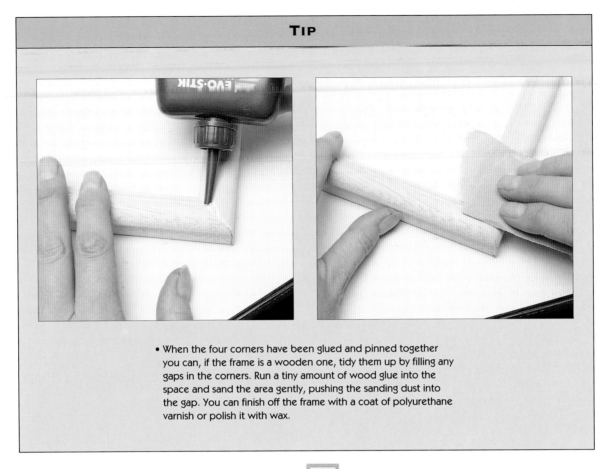

TIP

• When the four corners have been glued and pinned together you can, if the frame is a wooden one, tidy them up by filling any gaps in the corners. Run a tiny amount of wood glue into the space and sand the area gently, pushing the sanding dust into the gap. You can finish off the frame with a coat of polyurethane varnish or polish it with wax.

18 Use masking tape or brown gummed paper to cover the joins around the back, to help keep out insects and protect the picture from damp. A stamp roller is useful for moistening the gummed paper. Use a craft knife to trim off the ends of the tape or gummed paper.

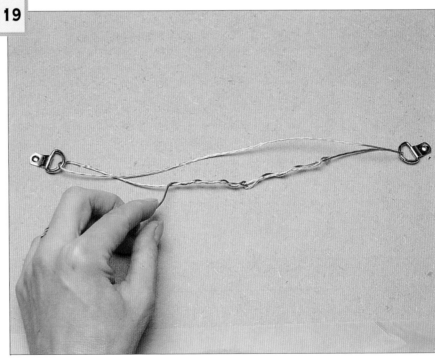

19 If you are using screw eyes rather than D-rings, insert them now, before attaching the wire or cord.

20

20 When it comes to painting the frame (see step 11) you can achieve great effects by matching one of the colors in the picture itself.

GLASS AND CLIP FRAME

This is a simple way of displaying small posters, postcards, children's drawings or photographs. It is best used with items that are not larger than about 24 x 24in because the clips exert pressure on the glass, and if the area of glass is too large it is likely to crack. This project uses plastic glass clips and a wooden frame. The picture has been floated on black, to give it a definite edge, and the wooden frame has been painted black to match.

You will need

◊ Plastic ruler and pencil
◊ Mounting card
◊ Craft knife
◊ Adhesive tape or double-sided tape
◊ Length of 1 x 1in wood molding (see page 5 for estimating quantity)
◊ Miter cutter and clamp
◊ Saw
◊ Wood glue
◊ Drill and small bit
◊ Small hammer and nail punch
◊ ¾in panel pins
◊ Wood filler
◊ Sandpaper and wet and dry papers
◊ Paint
◊ Glass
◊ T-square
◊ Felt-tipped pen
◊ Glass cutter
◊ Glass clips
◊ Hangers

1 Measure your print – ours was 14 x 11in – and add ¾in all round. Cut a piece of mounting card to this larger size.

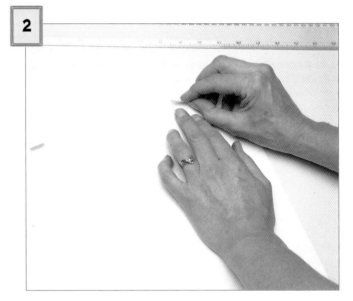

2 Use double-sided adhesive tape or make a hinge from ordinary adhesive tape to hold the picture in position on the mounting card. It is easier to move the picture if you make a mistake if it is held by a simple hinge rather than double-sided tape.

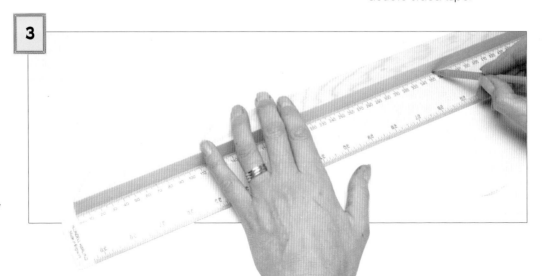

3 Cut the first angle on the frame, then measure along from the outside corner, using the long dimension first, and mark.

TIP

• If you are making a larger frame, use a piece of hardboard as a backing for the mounting card to give it extra strength.

4

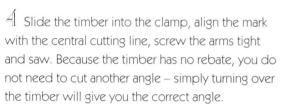

5

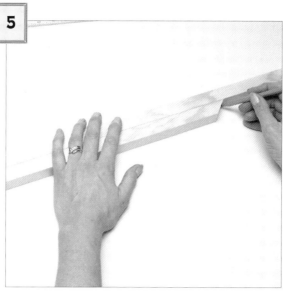

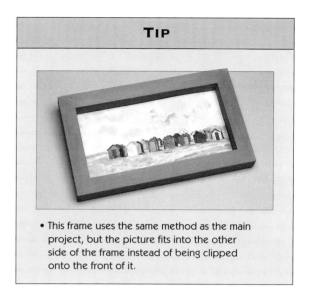
4 Slide the timber into the clamp, align the mark with the central cutting line, screw the arms tight and saw. Because the timber has no rebate, you do not need to cut another angle – simply turning over the timber will give you the correct angle.

5 Use the first cut piece to measure the second long side, placing them back to back and marking the outside corners. Cut the two shorter sides in the same way.

6

7

6 Apply some wood glue to one cut angle of a long side and place it in the clamp with a short side. Adjust and tighten when the angles sit neatly together.

7 Use a drill to make two small holes for the pins and drive them in, using a nail punch to drive them just below the level of the wood.

8

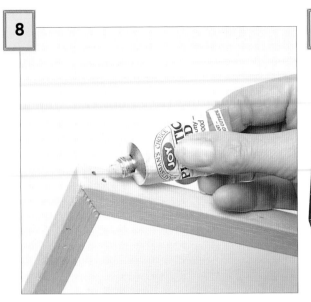

8 Fill the holes with wood filler, leave to dry and smooth with sandpaper.

9

9 Paint the frame to suit your picture. We used black to match the mounting card, but you could use a color that harmonizes with the picture you are framing or one that will complement your furnishings. Leave to dry.

10

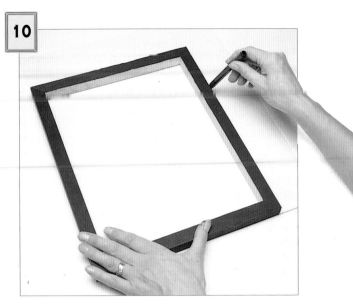

10 Use the finished frame as a guide to cut the glass. Lay the frame against a corner of the glass and mark the other two sides on the outside of the framewith a felt-tipped pen.

11

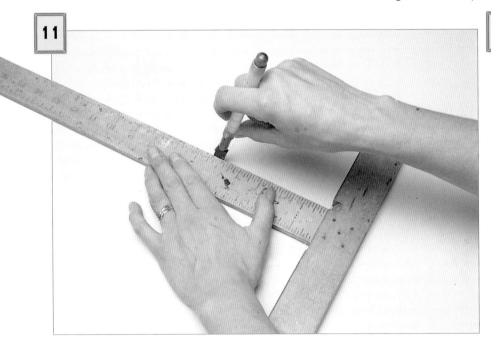

11 Use a wooden straight-edged ruler to cut the glass to size, then smooth the edges with wet and dry sandpaper, taking especial care at the corners. Clean the glass and sandwich the glass, the picture and the card. Lay them on the frame.

12

12 Use two glass clips on each side, making sure they are placed opposite each other. Mark the position of the holes in the clips all the way round and use the drill to make the holes. Screw the clips into position. The clips must be screwed sufficiently tightly to hold the glass securely but not so tightly that the glass cracks. Screw hangers in place on the back of the frame.

TIP

• The shops are full of frames made with metal clips and hardboard and they are so reasonably priced that you may not think it worthwhile to make your own, but they are a good way of using up the small pieces of glass and hardboard that are left over from larger projects. To make a frame with glass and metal clips, cut the hardboard to size, then cut the glass to exactly the same size. Smooth the edges of the glass. Fit D-rings to the hardboard, position the picture and slide on the metal clips, digging the metal legs into the back of the hardboard.

FABRIC AND PAPER FRAMES

Frames made in this way are ideal birthday and Christmas presents, and they are the perfect way of displaying all those school photographs that seem to accumulate.

You can use almost any paper you like – wrapping paper, hand-made paper or lightweight cotton. You might want to practice on some less expensive material before using hand-made paper, as we have done to make this double frame.

You will need
◊ Mounting card or equivalent
◊ Plastic ruler and pencil
◊ Mount cutter
◊ Polyester wadding
◊ Clear, all-purpose adhesive
◊ Sharp-pointed scissors
◊ Hand-made paper or fabric to cover frames
◊ Double-sided adhesive tape

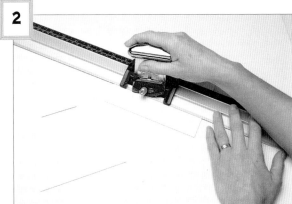

1 Cut four pieces of card. In our example the outside measurements of each are 6½ x 5⅛in. You will also need to cut a piece of card 6⅛in long by ⅛in wide, which will form the spine of the frame.

2 In two of the larger rectangles of card cut a window; ours measured 3¼ x 2⅛in. (See page 11 for using a mount cutter.)

3 Cut two pieces of wadding to the same size as the window mounts and use a small amount of adhesive to glue them to the fronts of the mounts.

4

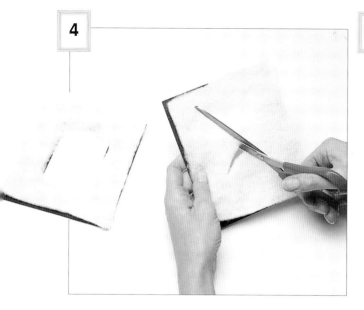

4 Use sharp scissors to snip a hole in the center of the wadding, then trim away the excess to the edge of the window.

5

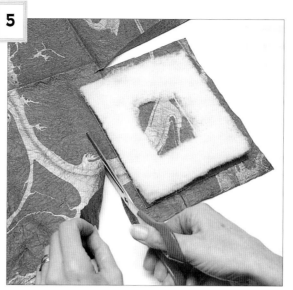

5 Cut one piece of hand-made paper for the back – ours measured 13½ x 7⅛in – and two pieces for the front – ours measured 7½ x 6¾in.

6

6 Put the larger piece of paper on your working surface with the wrong side upward. Lay the two backing cards on it so that there is ⅜in between them. Glue the thin strip of card into this space. Apply adhesive around the edges of the paper and carefully and neatly stick it over the card, working on the top and bottom edges first before turning in the sides. Pull the paper tightly over the edges so that it is taut all round. Trim the corners so that the paper lies neatly and flat.

7

7 Cut a strip of covering paper to cover the spine and glue it into position. Put aside until the adhesive is completely dry.

8

8 Take the two smaller pieces of paper and place them, wrong sides upward, on the working surface. Lay the window mounts on this so that an even amount of paper shows all round. Glue down the paper all the way round, making sure that it is taut and that the corners are neat.

9

9 With the back of the mount toward you, use sharp scissors to make a hole in the center of the mount. Make four cuts, just up to, but not right into, the corners.

10

11

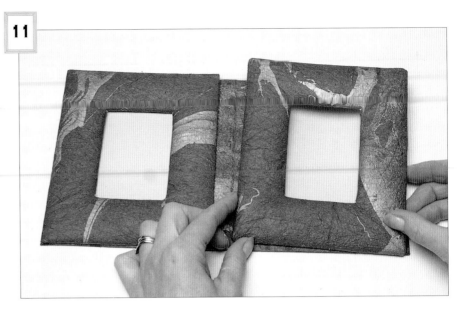

10 Trim off the excess triangles of paper and glue and fold the inside edges, making sure that the front edges are neat and that there are no creases, especially in the corners. Trim off any excess paper or, if you have used fabric, any loose threads and frayed edges.

11 Use double-sided adhesive tape to stick the two front sections carefully to the back, leaving the top open so that you can slide in the photograph.

DOUBLE WOOD FRAME

This is the ideal frame for small pictures such as photographs or postcards. Because the fine inner frame is used in combination with a wider outer frame, the picture can be shown to advantage without having to use a mount.

You will need

◊ Narrow wood molding (see page 5 for estimating quantity)
◊ Plastic ruler and pencil
◊ Miter cutter and clamp
◊ Saw
◊ Craft knife
◊ Wood glue
◊ Drill and fine bit
◊ Panel pins
◊ Small hammer
◊ Wide wood molding but with no rebate (see page 5 for estimating quantity)
◊ Nail punch
◊ White emulsion
◊ Acrylic paints
◊ ⅟₁₆in glass
◊ T-square
◊ Felt-tipped pen
◊ Glass cutter
◊ ⅟₁₆in hardboard
◊ Screw eyes
◊ Wire or card

1 Measure the photograph and assemble the frame from the narrow molding as described in the Basic Frame (see page 14).

2 Use the completed inner frame to determine the dimensions of the outside frame. This is made from timber with no rebate. We used timber that was 1¼ x ¼in.

3 Make the first miter cut, then make the two long sides and the short sides as described in the instructions for the Glass and Clip Frame (see page 20). Again this molding has no rebate.

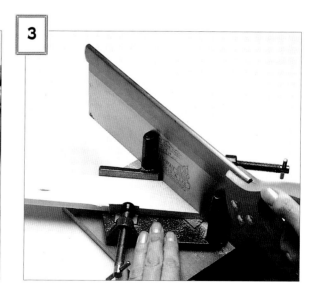

4

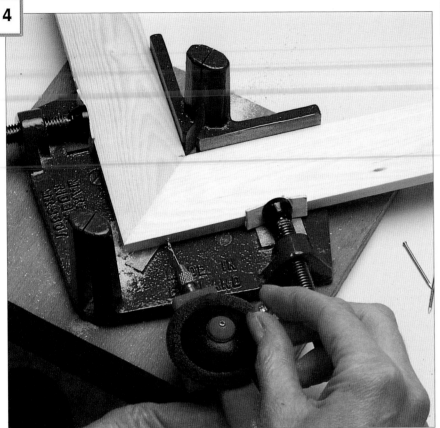

4 Glue and clamp the first corner together, then drill holes for the panel pins; we used 1in pins, but you must use a size that will hold both pieces of wood securely. Use a nail punch to drive the pins in straight.

5

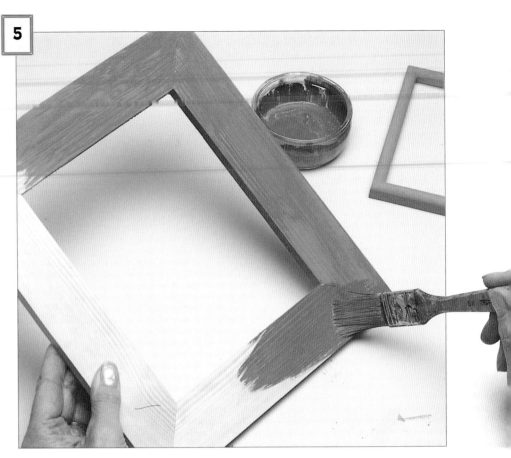

5 Paint the frames. Use contrasting colors for the frames, mixing acrylic paints with white emulsion until you find shades you like. Experiment on pieces of scrap wood before you paint the frame itself.

6

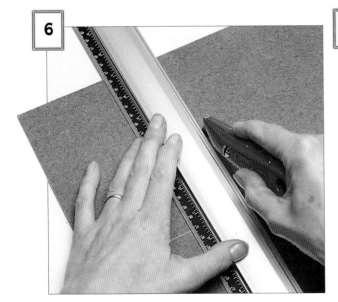

6 Cut the glass and a piece of hardboard to size, using the inner frame as a guide as to the dimensions. Fit the glass, picture, hardboard and inner frame together.

7

7 Hold the hardboard in place by driving some panel pins carefully into the edge of the inner frame.

8

8 Apply wood glue to the inside edge of the outer frame and push the inner frame through from the back. It should fit neatly. Insert the screw eyes and attach the wire so that you can hang your picture up.

BOX FRAME

This kind of frame is useful for holding three-dimensional objects such as a piece of embroidery or collectable items such as badges or medals. There are several ways of making box frames, but this is a simple and effective method. The size of the frame is determined by the backing board, which can be covered with colored card or with polyester wadding and fabric. We have made the frame to display an arrangement of dried flowers mounted on card.

You will need

◊ Hardboard
◊ Plastic ruler and pencil
◊ Craft knife
◊ Polyester wadding
◊ Scissors
◊ Fabric
◊ Clear, all-purpose adhesive
◊ 1in hockey wood molding (see page 5 for estimating quantity)
◊ Miter cutter and clamp
◊ Saw
◊ Wood glue
◊ Drill and fine bit
◊ Panel pins
◊ Small hammer
◊ ⅛in glass
◊ Glass cutter
◊ T-square
◊ Card
◊ Masking tape or brown gummed paper
◊ Screw eyes
◊ Wire or cord

1 Cut a piece of hardboard to size – we used a piece that is 12⅛ x 8⅛in. Cover the hardboard with polyester wadding and cut a piece of fabric that is about ⅛in larger all round than the hardboard.

2 Stretch the fabric over the wadding and glue it firmly to the back, making sure that the corners are neatly mitered.

3 Cut the first miter in the molding and, working on a long side first, measure the covered hardboard. Transfer this measurement to the outside edge of the molding, measuring from one corner to the other.

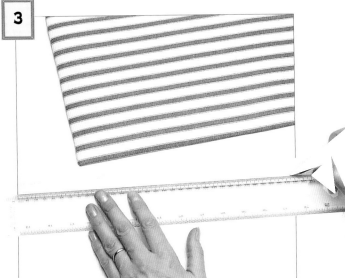

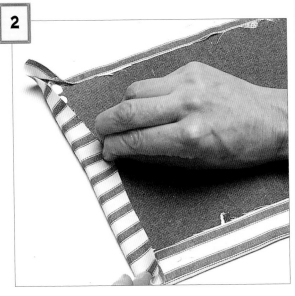

4

4 Slide the molding into the miter clamp and align the mark with the center line of the vice. Cut the remaining three sides and assemble the frame as described in the instructions for the Basic Frame (see page 14). Once the frame is complete, cut a piece of glass to fit neatly inside the frame. Lay the frame face down on the table, clean the glass carefully and fit it into the frame.

5

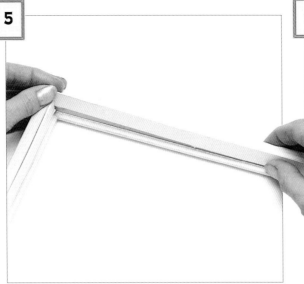

5 Measure the depth of the side from the glass to the back of the frame – in our frame this was ⅜in – and cut four strips of thick card to this width and long enough to fit along the inside of the frame. Glue them in place, sticking the long pieces down first. These strips of card will hold the glass in position at the front of the box.

6

6 Attach the object or objects to the covered backing board. We used all-purpose adhesive to hold the card in place.

7

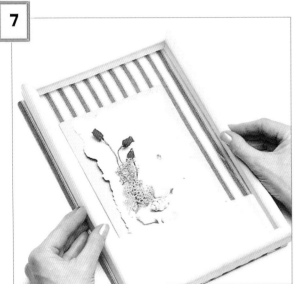

7 Place the frame over the backing board and carefully over the box.

8

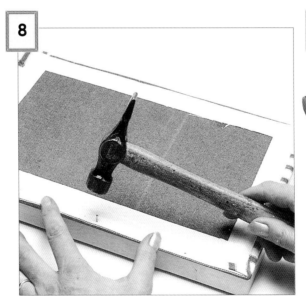

8 Use small panel pins, tapped through the backing board into the frame, to hold the back in place. Cover the join with strips of masking tape or brown gummed paper.

9

9 With your hand drill, make holes, about one-third of the way down, on each side of the frame and insert the screw eyes. Attach wire or cord for hanging.

SHELL FRAME

If you have an old wooden frame that has seen better days, you can completely revitalize it by covering it with shells, feathers or even small bits of seaweed. Alternatively you can make your own frame, although you will need to use a fairly flat molding or one that has only a gentle curve.

You will need
◊ Wooden frame
◊ White emulsion paint
◊ Acrylic paint
◊ Wire wool or a rag
◊ White candle (optional for wax resist)
◊ Screw eyes
◊ Mirror
◊ Panel pins and hammer
◊ Masking tape or gummed brown paper
◊ Strong adhesive
◊ Interior wall filler (optional for curved frame)
◊ Gold paint

1 If the frame is going to be painted, apply a coat of white emulsion and leave to dry.

2 Mix the acrylic paint, diluting it with a little emulsion to give a smooth, runny consistency. Experiment until you have a shade you like. Paint the frame and before the paint is completely dry use wire wool or a rag to drag some of the paint off.

3 An alternative method is to use the end of a candle to draw patterns on the dried base coat.

4 When you apply the acrylic paint, the wax will resist the paint and leave the white base coat showing through.

5

5 Screw the eyes into the back of the frame and, if you wish, insert the mirror, holding it in place with small panel pins. Cover the join with masking tape or gummed paper. Use a fairly strong adhesive to stick the shells and other ornaments into position. If the frame has a very uneven profile you may find it easier to mix a small amount of interior wall filler to press the shells into.

6 When you are happy with the final arrangement of the shells, add a touch of gold tube paint to create highlights on the shells, wiping off any excess before it dries.

6

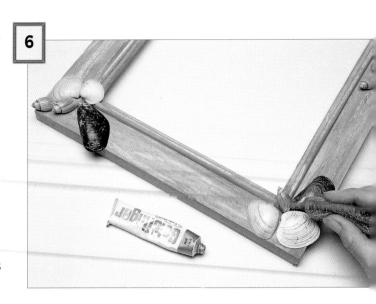

REVIVING AN OLD FRAME

You might come across an attractive old frame in a junk shop or on a second-hand stall, but, when you get it home you realize that not only is it in a worse state than you at first thought but it also will not fit the picture you intended to put in it. You can use your newly acquired skills to take the frame apart and remake it with new glass so that it fits perfectly.

You will need
◊ Pliers
◊ Hammer
◊ Screwdriver
◊ Plastic ruler and pencil
◊ Miter cutter and clamp
◊ Saw
◊ Craft knife
◊ Wood glue
◊ Drill and fine bit
◊ Panel pins
◊ Fine wire wool
◊ Emulsion paint
◊ Gold paint (in liquid, powder or tube form)
◊ ⅛in glass
◊ Glass cutter
◊ T-square
◊ Masking tape or brown gummed paper
◊ Screw eyes
◊ Wire or cord

1

$\mathbb{1}$ First remove the backing and the glass from the old frame. Take care because the glass may be old and fragile. Stand the frame on a corner, hold the opposite corner and gently push down until the corners crack.

TIP

- If the frame is an old wooden one, always sand and stain it before applying a wax finish.
- Make a plain frame by applying two coats of a solid, dark paint.

2

$\mathbb{2}$ If pins have been used, push the sides apart and wiggle them apart. If the frame has been underpinned, use a screwdriver and hammer to drive the pins out.

3

$\mathbb{3}$ Once the frame is in pieces, use your pliers to remove any remaining pins. Working on one of the long sides, cut a new mitered corner.

4

4 Measure the long side of the picture you want to frame and transfer the measurement to the inside of the newly cut side.

5

5 Slide the molding into the miter clamp and align the mark with the center cutting line. Cut all the sides as for the Basic Frame (see page 14) and reassemble the pieces.

6

6 You can now decorate the frame, choosing a style that is in keeping with the picture that is going in it. We have used an old print of some frogs and want the frame to look suitably distressed and aged. To achieve this appearance, rub the frame all over with fine wire wool.

7

7 Apply a coat of dark brick-red emulsion all over the frame. Leave to dry. You may need to apply a second coat if the first did not cover the frame completely.

8

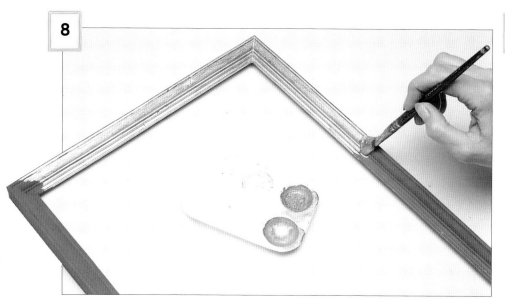

9

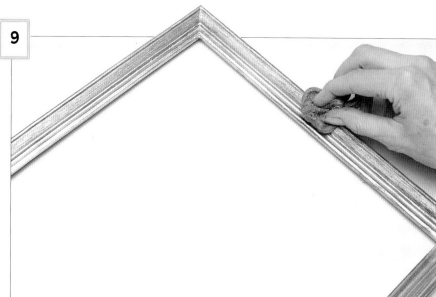

8 When the paint is dry, smooth it carefully with fine wire wool, then apply a coat of liquid gold leaf or another proprietary gold paint. Some gold powders need to be mixed with shellac or button polish, so always check the manufacturer's instructions.

9 When the gold paint is dry, rub it gently with fine wire wool to give a distressed look, with the red paint showing through in places. Insert the glass and finish off the frame as described in the instructions for the Basic Frame (see page 18).

PAPIER-MÂCHÉ FRAME

Making this frame for a mirror will allow you to combine your framing skills with the satisfying craft of papier-mâché. We have created a simple design, with fish swimming around the glass, although this is a technique that allows you to give your creative talents full rein.

You will need

◊ ⅛ x ⅛in plain wooden molding (see page 5 for estimating quantity)
◊ Plastic ruler and pencil
◊ Miter cutter and clamp
◊ Saw
◊ Craft knife
◊ Wood glue
◊ Drill and fine bit
◊ Panel pins
◊ Small hammer
◊ Tracing paper
◊ Mounting card or thick card
◊ Scraps of newspaper, torn into small pieces
◊ Masking tape
◊ Flour-and-water paste or wallpaper paste
◊ Masking tape or brown gummed paper
◊ Acrylic glue (optional)
◊ Clear, all-purpose adhesive
◊ White tissue paper
◊ Acrylic paint
◊ Polyurethane
◊ Screw eyes
◊ Wire or cord

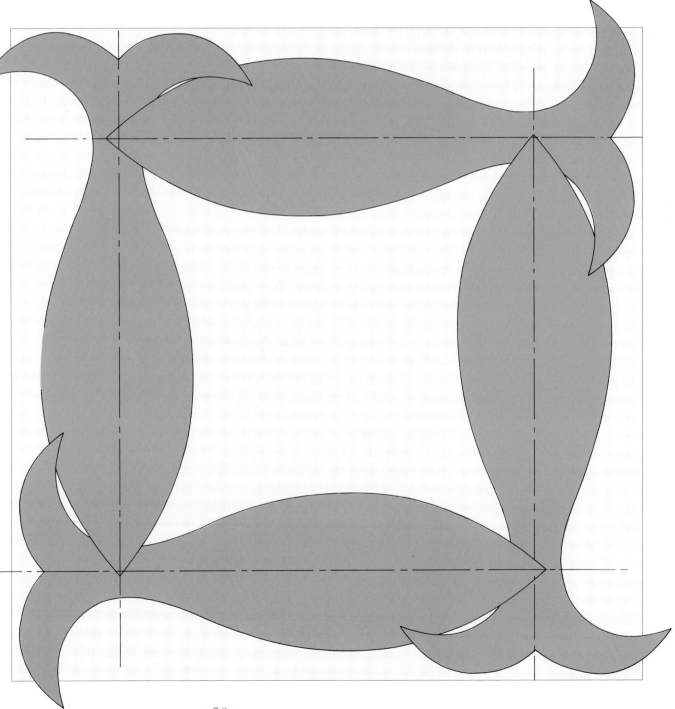

1

1 Use the wooden molding to make a three-sided frame, following the instructions for the Basic Frame (see page 14). We have made a square frame, measuring 6½ x 6½in. Leave the opening at the top so that you can slip in the mirror.

2

2 Trace the fish design (or a motif of your choice) onto a spare piece of card. Use a craft knife to cut out four fish shapes.

3

3 Tear up some pieces of newspaper and scrunch them up loosely. Use tape to hold them onto the parts of the fish bodies that you want to be fuller and more rounded.

4

4 Mix the paste. If you use flour-and-water paste you can add a small amount of acrylic glue to make it stronger. Dip pieces of paper into the paste and begin to cover the fish bodies. Do not let the paper become saturated with paste, and if you find that the paper is too wet, lay some dry pieces over the shapes. When you are satisfied with the overall shapes, smooth the surface of each fish and leave them somewhere warm until they are absolutely dry.

5

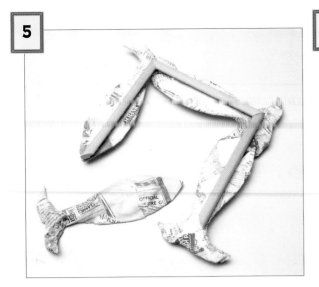

5 Take the frame and arrange the fish on it. When you are satisfied with the positions they are in, use a lot of adhesive to stick them, nose to tail, around the frame.

6

6 The fish at the top should be attached by its nose and tail. Place under a weight and leave until the adhesive is dry. Check that the mirror will slide into the frame, but do not leave it there yet. Add more layers of papier-mâché to the fish, using strips of paper across the back of the top fish to make sure it is firmly attached to its neighbors. Put back in a warm place to dry.

7

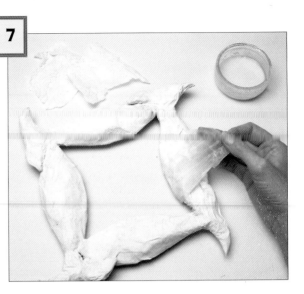

7 To finish the fish, cover them completely with two layers of white tissue paper. The colors of the paint will be much brighter and clearer if they are applied over a white base.

8

8 When the fish are dry, paint them in colors of your choice. Leave the paint to dry, then apply a coat of clear polyurethane.

9

9 Insert the mirror and apply screw eyes on the sides to hang up the frame.

GILDED AND PAINTED FRAME

Naive paintings and prints usually have a strong image, often in good, clear colors, and they do not usually need a mount if they are in a wide frame. We have chosen to frame a print of a sheep, which measures 16 x 12in. This frame can either be simply painted or it can be finished with gold to give it extra sparkle.

You will need
◊ Molding (see page 5 for estimating quantity)
◊ Miter cutter and clamp
◊ Saw
◊ Plastic ruler and pencil
◊ Wood glue
◊ Drill and fine bit
◊ Panel pins
◊ Small hammer
◊ Nail punch
◊ Shellac and paintbrush (optional)
◊ Red emulsion paint
◊ Fine wire wool
◊ Masking tape
◊ Emulsion and acrylic paints
◊ Gold paint (in liquid, powder or tube form)
◊ Shoe polish and soft cloth (optional)
◊ Metal gold leaf and size
◊ Soft, long-handled brush

1 Make the frame in the molding of your choice, following the instructions for the Basic Frame (see page 14). If you wish, seal the wood by applying a coat of shellac. Apply two or three coats of red paint, leaving each coat to dry completely before you paint on the next. Gently rub the surface with fine wire wool.

TIP
• If you need to tone a color down, add a little black acrylic paint rather than more of the base color.

2 If you are going to have a gilded edge, apply strips of masking tape around the center of the frame.

3 Mix the emulsion and acrylic paints. We used dark green, made by mixing green acrylic with a little white emulsion paint to give it body. Apply the paint to the outer edge of the frame, taking care that it does not seep under the masking tape.

4

4 When the paint is completely dry, rub it gently with wire wool to distress it. If you wish you can leave the frame as it is.

5

5 If you want to add a gold edge, remove the masking tape and put new strips of tape over the area you have just painted. Following the manufacturer's instructions for the gold paint you are using, paint the edge of the frame and leave this to dry.

6

6 If you want the gold to look "aged", apply a tiny amount of dark shoe polish and rub it carefully with a soft cloth. If you prefer, use wire wool to remove part of the gold to give an even more distressed appearance.

7

7 If you prefer, you can apply quick gilding with metal gold leaf, which is quick and easy to use. Apply fresh strips of masking tape as in step 5. Working on small sections of the frame, apply some gilding size and wait until it becomes tacky.

8

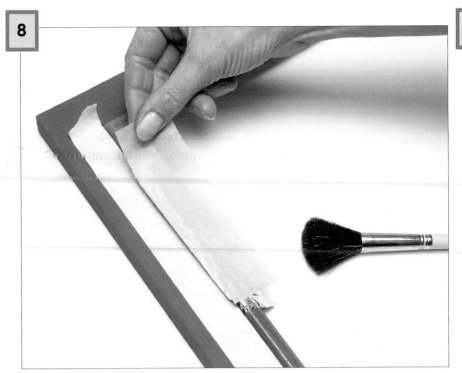

8 Cut a piece of gold leaf large enough to cover the edge and leave the paper backing on it. Use your fingertips to carefully position the gold leaf and to press it down gently.

9

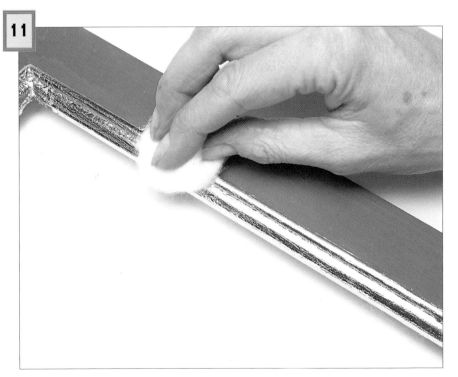

9 You may find it helpful to use a soft brush to make sure you have pressed it down completely. Carefully remove the backing paper.

10

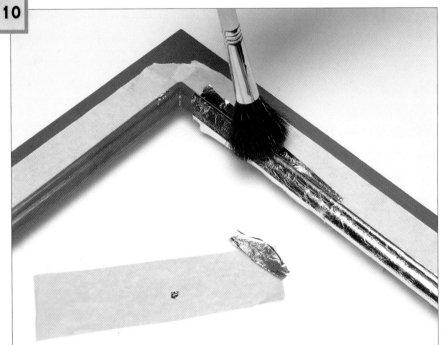

10 Continue to work around the frame, overlapping the gold leaf by about ⅛in each time. If you find you have missed any, use small scraps of gold leaf to cover the gaps or, when the size has dried completely, use gold paint to fill in the gaps. Use a soft, long-handled brush to remove any loose particles.

11 Leave to dry for a few hours or, ideally, overnight until the size is quite dry. Use a ball of cotton wool to buff the gold leaf until it gleams.

TIP

• When it comes to the corners, take care not to overlap the gold leaf too much, otherwise they will be very bulky. Again, use a soft brush to remove loose particles.

FRAMING AN OIL PAINTING

Oil paintings need to be treated rather differently from prints and watercolors, but it is still important to have a space between the image and the frame. A simple way of doing this is to float the painting on a board covered in a material such as hessian or coarse linen. The fabric is stretched taut over hardboard and the painting is fixed to the covered board. An alternative method, which we are using, is to make an inner slip and an outside frame. The slip can be wood, gold or silver or, as we used, linen, and it serves the additional purpose of holding the glass slightly away from the surface of the painting if you choose to glaze it, although traditionally oil paintings are not glazed.

You will need
◊ Ruler and pencil
◊ Linen slip molding (see page 5 for estimating quantity)
◊ Masking tape
◊ Miter cutter and clamp
◊ Saw
◊ Wood glue
◊ Drill and fine bit
◊ Panel pins
◊ Small hammer
◊ Nail punch
◊ Outer molding (see page 5 for estimating quantity)
◊ D-rings or screw eyes
◊ Wire or cord

1 Measure the painting. Ours was 23 x 17in. Working on the long measurement first, add about ⅛in and cut a piece of linen slip molding to this length. To protect the linen and to stop it from tearing, cover the cutting area with masking tape before cutting.

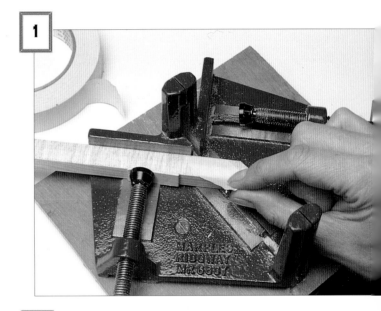

2 Follow the instructions for making the Basic Frame (see page 14), but before you drill the holes for the panel pins lay the pieces around the oil painting, holding them together in position to check that the frame will fit. Oil paintings are not always perfectly square and you may need to make some fine adjustments.

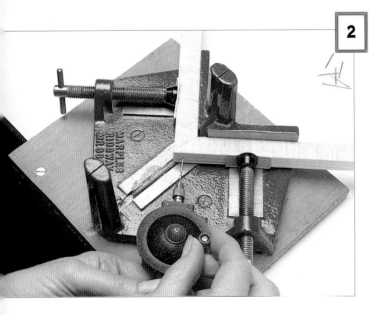

3 Finish off the frame as described on page 18. Use a nail punch to drive the panel pins into the corners, making sure that they are securely held.

4

5

6

4 Make the outer frame, using the inner frame as a guide to mark the measurements. Do not allow any extra because the frames should fit tightly together. Make the outer frame as the inner frame.

5 Fit the oil painting into the slip frame and carefully insert panel pins to hold it in place. Place the outer frame over the slip frame. Pin the back by driving panel pins in upright then tapping them until they bend over. You will need two or three pins along each side.

6 Make holes for the screw eyes or D-rings on each side of the outer frame.